Praise for As For the Body: Annotations of an Owner's Manual

"This text has a divine awareness of the tension of itself. The tension of what a body is vs. how it is perceived in private/public spheres. & this text is a rejection of that awareness—awareness as a type of labeling, a language that attempts to box or understand. Blake Marcelle does not ask the reader to understand, but to ask: can there be a belief system built of the body? Religion of the west forces us to extricate the body, throw it down a well to soak & swell with the sin of the underground, of the mother. What do we worship instead, when the body is left to rot? Some find the holy in substances that erode the body faster, like a storm surge against a fragile cliff. Some find our gaze not on the lord, but on the scraps cast on the perimeter of the churchyard. The remnants of beings deemed too angry or outrageous or in-between to attend ceremony. How does one escape without collapsing into the sea? Where can these beings go to worship their rusted edges? Blake creates a temple of the body as the body—diagraming the violence that occurs in the realization of body as commodity, to reclamation of body as possibility. Of infinite. As Blake writes, this is an unlearning. A "learning, / again and slowly/ with my hands, how to allow for the weather/ without clean socks. And half the dirty tea cups."

-**Shawnie Hamer**

"Blake Marcelle's poetry takes up the difficult task of cataloging the rages and forgivenesses of the body. With a furtive attention to detail, they explore a topography of personal and cultural memory, layering the sacred and the profane, the honest and the apocryphal, the wild and the ordinary, willing and inventing a new freedom. AS FOR THE BODY is a fearless, full-lunged big-hearted debut.

-**Mindy Nettifee**

AS FOR THE BODY:
Annotation of an Owner's Manual

Blake Marcelle

Punch Drunk Press Ltd.
Denver, Colorado

Punch Drunk Press Ltd.
PO Box 9435
Denver CO 80209

Interior Design: Blake Marcelle, Brice Maiurro
Photography: Michael Benko
Cover Text Design: Jona Fine

Library of Congress Control Number:
9780998890227

Marcelle, Blake

As for The Body: Annotations of an Owner's Manual / Blake Marcelle 1st Ed.

ISBN – 978-0-9988902-2-7

PUNCH DRUNK PRESS

PUNCH DRUNK PRESS LTD
DENVER, CO

To my little brother, Luca, for listening when I talk in my sleep.

To my best friend, Lije, for opening the closet door and being there when I came out.

To my sister, Bee, for being everything you are and for the endless love and support.

To my parents, for always encouraging me to write. I hope you understand how much I love you.

AS FOR THE BODY:
Annotations of an Owner's Manual

BLAKE MARCELLE

An imprint of Punch Drunk Press Ltd.

CONTENTS:

NOTES ON BECOMING:

Of the body, I will say
Only that I have little endurance
For its fits and starts.
As a mother reminisces on herself
As she was,
Without the joy and plunder a child brings,
I remember, fondly,
Some imagined other,
Existing without,
Or else outside of,
Or else consumed by
And oblivious to the body
With its ambient rage.

What would I sacrifice,
Now,
For some perfect separation
Of the objective and the flesh-bound?

Here,
Waiting, I suppose,
For a possibility of growth
As reverse transubstantiation,
This awful hideous thing
To become verbal,
To abandon its nature
For a firm belief
In ritual signification,
In the word as flesh,
Flesh as metaphor,
Balkanization of the real
As the reclamation of some holy city,
Or else as it's becoming occupied,
Given over for the price of bread and circuses.

Of the body,
I will say,
I did not want to know.

TOUT CE QUI VIENT AVANT ET APRÈS:

There is a hideous softness
That attacks me some evenings.

It finds the clutter in my desk:
Old gum wrappers and crumpled receipts,

The undone resolutions:
Drink three glasses of water every day,
Learn French,
Wear matching socks,

The split ends,
Sweaty palms,
And stale restlessness.

And it forgives.
Like a self-help book convert,
Like an answer-eyed priest,
Like a human body.

*Gender Dysphoria
MUSCLED:

In the mirror,
Throwing words at a face,
Not fitting,
Wondering if this jaw has widened,
If perception is a setter of bones.

Remembering my name,
Not fitting,
My voice says it aloud.
(Hear: "Requiem for the signified."
Hear: "New names are for those
Who have claimed a solution
To the problem of a body -
Their victory for long nights
And difficult revisions.")

My chest, tightly bound,
The obtrusive flesh,
A recluse,
Pulled closer.
(Hear: dismemberment.)
My voice, a grandmother's voice,
Aloud: "Will I always be a stranger?"

There are no words,
Not fitting,
Guttural, slow:
Has my jaw widened,
Chest bound tightly?

Understand, now
That this is not for you,
That I have shirked
The imagination of a sacred duty
To offer the clarity of my shame
As a translation,
As a balm,
As solidarity,
That I do not know you.

"Surely," says the girl,
(Hear: Alice)
"I must've been changed
In the night."

"No," says the boy.
(Hear: nothing).

The girl,
Her memories,
Have they widened,
Bound tightly?
(Hear: "becoming," "undone,"
Hear: requiem for a reflection in old photographs).

The boy,
Aloud: "Is she dead?"
The girl,
Aloud: "Balkanized, monstrous."
(Hear: nothing).

HANGUPS, FEATURING 'FIGHT CLUB' and OCD:

1. Is afraid of all bugs.
Butterflies are no exception.

2. Grinds teeth loudly
When people try to reclaim the word
"Cunt."

3. Finds the word "irksome" irksome.
Does not enjoy the irony.

4. Spells the words "s-a-t-a-n," "p-e-n-t-a-g-r-a-m," and "d-e-m-o-n,"
While feeling criticized by the punk world.

5. Feels overinflated/situationally inappropriate amounts of shame
For saying "punk world."

6. Believes that the first rule of being a poet is that you don't talk about
being a poet.

7. Sings in public but experiences sense of violation when heard
Singing in the shower.

8. Sees list poems as a cop out.

COMPOSITE MEMORY:

I drifted fitfully
On the train
Passing Poughkeepsie,
Recalled in a halfsleep
A dream I had
Years ago -

Something about mothers
And coffee shops
A salt shaker?
Paper coffee sleeves?

It felt like I was waiting long.

Old women?
Same dream?
Yes
And somehow
It is important
That it was
Not filling in details
In blank space -

Synthesizing every dream
With mothers
Coffee shops
Feelings of waiting

No — I wasn't waiting.

I was late.

FIELD GUIDE (ONE):

We write the bricks and mortars,
Our words for them.
After all, the real things
Were graffitied,
Storefronts notwithstanding
Rocks, the actual things,
Not the names.

And I am trying out
New monikers
For you,
As well:
Prosody, plum juice,
Extended-release Ani DiFranco,
Placebo-Panacea,
Tall.

FIELD GUIDE (TWO):

Of course,
Resentfully,
Everything would fall
Apart
(A distance and not a designation)
In Spring's doorway,
Rendering the protective layers
Of winter
Too obvious,

Heat rash across my shoulders,
Thrown away in exchange
For a strange revelation of you,
The name more than the thing,
Still,
All liquid skin.

FIELD GUIDE (THREE):

The museum of this is sparse,
Too much air and quiet,
Clean in the modern sense.
To my left, cigarette cartons stacked
Dominoes,
Mostly Marlboro.
Behind the velvet rope,
A small house,
A doll house full of mismatched earrings.
An awkward choreography,
I do not know how to fold my hands,
Anymore.

Best attempts
Are a tango
Locked at the hips,
Jeans too tight,
In the embrace of my own solipsisms.

Gospels have dried up,
Leaving the river bed:
A stark reminder
Of the cold,
the clean,
their absence.
Sitting in the crevice,
I push the dust and clay
Through my hair
And over my skin,
Hoping it will somehow become
Flood.

In Karnataka,
The truck beds are open,
Flowers piled high,
Tumbling into the crowded street,
Offerings for the shrine
Giving themselves up
To the traffic to be trampled,
All fragrance and oil,

All wilt and browned,
Like a cut apple,
Caramelizing,
Half a mile away from the home of the Gods,
Wasting themselves, brazenly,
On the universe.

The dark Cathedral in Naples
Is packed with devotees
Of Black Madonna,
All knee bend and hand clasp,
Waiting for her to emerge from the marble,
Decalcify her beatific face
And become from stone,
Like water,
Struck by the staff of Moses.
They are satisfied, why-ever,
To go home and pay the rent
On their bodies
With familiar motions.

It is enough, certainly,
To have come from dust,
Themselves,
To plant olive trees,
Lemon trees,
Something.

ANACHRONISM PT. 1:

Allowing yourself to be bent
By the texture of Tuesday afternoon
(A stucco wall),
Your father's restlessness
(A family heirloom),
Hold it tightly.
Run your thumb over the brass.
His restlessness is a pocket watch,
A typewriter key
(The letter Q)
Sticking with lack of use.

BUDDHIST HORROR MOVIE:

1. A young atheist, I went on a sort of spiritual bar crawl, begging holy men to tell me what God tasted like, to give me the pink of a Divine Lung (just one), enough to stumble
home on and wake up in the afternoon with a heathen apologetics hangover, Jesus Juice vomit sticky on my chin.

2. All day I've been mourning the texture of motion, impulse entreating me to indulge in the muscle-memorized fear of gracelessness, lack of capacity - as a child, compelled to grip each small vision in the plastic kaleidoscope before it is disrupted and reformed, lost to motion.

3. The moon is communion-wafer-pale,embittering with its fragility. A petulant toddler, I still jones for the milk
of twin illusions: opacity and permanence.

LYING IS NOT A METAPHOR:

While on vacation
In the outskirts of moral hubris,
My apologies took up amateurish architecture,
A way of busying themselves
In my two weeks of absence.
They became mass producers of confessional booths,
Building little wooden boxes
In the exit wound of my mouth
Where, "sorry," became the truth:

"I am essentially you
At seven years old,
Pretending sleep in the backseat
Of your mother's maroon Buick
Every afternoon in July, 1998,
Because we all want
Something to see the shameless Tired in us
And manage not to abuse all that comes with it:
The Small,
The defenseless,
The heavy.

So, I woke up
In your bed this morning
Ready to say I was sorry,
That last night had been maximum-security prison crowd-surfing,
Had been swallowing a mosh pit
Full of versions of myself
That look better with the lights off,
Had been a manic episode after a visit to the arms dealer,
Had been a shitty acid trip
Where I hallucinated patterns in my chaos
And balconies three feet past the edge
Of every cliff in a fifty-mile radius,
Only to realize that left out everything:

The everything where I pulled my pulse out
Like a shitty ballistics timer,
The everything where you didn't need to tell me
That broken stopwatches aren't worth MI-7 synchronizing,

The everything where I lay in your bed
Trying to saltwater-tumble the jagged out of my breathing,
Forgetting that the equation for smooth
Is saltwater plus motion plus time.

I awoke to a piece of you that couldn't metabolize metaphors
Or accept my knee-jerk desire
To repay gentleness with Lucky Strikes,
Reverse-bumming my way out of karma
Even though I know the work to be done,
Know how to pull back covers for you
On the Worst Nights
Where we sleep adjacent
Like twin brothers,
Matching snot-noses and Hulk pajamas.

It comes down to innocence and confusion,
How I wake up
Somewhere in the goldmine
Of Colorado fall,
Numbed toes,
Morning smokes
Blurred dizzyingly into the remnants
Of slow-release sleep aid.

How ramshackle-easy
Everything hardens back into place,
Jaw-muscling and breakaway-vaceing
After spit-take Tuesdays,
Bananarchy bicycling,
Bookmarked pages and chocolate bars.

Would you believe me
If I told you that I may forget
Tomorrow or by half past three,
But right now, I know exactly what we are doing here?

FREE BIN:

We swap binary artifacts
In the living room,
Trading pretty reckless bits
Of repression drag
That turn into Christmas morning
On our "wrong bodies;"
Fitting corsets to new bloom
Skittle tits
And button fly boxers
To Venus flytraps,
Muscle shirts for smooth arms,
Shaving cream for the girls
Who got blue announcements,
Jackson Pollocks on every wall
For the splatter-frames/
Boxes full of boxes/
Cubist queers;
Tracing erasure burns with sharpie,
Calling suspenders "our dapper,"
My old lipstick their "brash sexy,"
My stitches "her new shoelaces,"
His hand-me-down butch-babe button-ups
Fit me just right.

Not gay as in happy,
Not queer as in fuck you.
Queer as in kaleidoscopes
Full of broken glass,
As in swagger in every pocket,
As in mascara and muscle,
As in gender-bender paperclips
Picking the locks
On pixie sticks and particularities.

As in glitter on your boots,
As in teach me bowties
And I'll teach you boyfriends
And we'll take turns shadowboxing
The toxic masculine bare fisted / borne teeth.

Queer as in asexual fort building,
As in problematic
Is everything but the dogs,
As in made up words for
"God damn! You look good!,"
As in your skin fits,
Borrow mine if ya get cold.

As an invitation
To tell me your real name:
The one invisible inked on the back of your neck
That you've read lemon-juiced and backwards
In the mirror all those years.

*Sexual Assault
TURMERIC:

The day after the a.c. broke
Open in the   heat
Filled the room of clapboard house
With turmeric smoke
Slapstick walls sweating profusely
        Nauseously nervously
    The holy unbearable claustrophobic
        Mason-Dixon summer
        Crawled under my sheets
        Molesting my mind
With humid hands

And in the morning the children
    Had parents
The strangers
    Had palms
And there were obvious paperback bibles
    In the backs
Of disappointed pickup trucks

Hungry busy salty exhaustion
Threatening stomach and shoulders
Forearms with promises of fidelity

I slept sudden   desperate
Like projectile vomiting
Into bed   facedown
In sweaty stagnation
Crescents of the sugarsound
Aggression
Of canonized
Patience in the pale of my wrist
        Almost forceful
        A cannibalistic ritual
        Of anger eating anger

Brain condensates in this scorch
Dripping   cloudy juices
Out of my sinus cavity
        Washing lips

Muscles evaporate

16

Nostalgic for the human
Sturdiness of winter
Graciously offering something
To steel ourselves against
    To bite down on
      Fantasies almost sexual
      Of cool blue tile
While the roomless house
Pulses sticky warm traps
With wall-to-wall carpeting
Building the world thick
As a spoiled milkshake

And my mother feels us rusting
Four rivers south
Of the well-lit kitchen
    Backdrop of frequent stress dreams
      Where tomatoes turn to bloody beef
      In my closed mouth
Where the table and I swivel
Sob & vomit
Delirious with earnest shocked
Guilty disgust
      Pins and needles of panicked betrayal

Pungent pheromones drip
Steady and insistent
   River down the venerable sidewalks
And glitter - drinkably seductive
Under the totalitarian afternoon

Boxes of books go stale
Upstairs   heat opening
The pulp   making the pages porous
Chapters accosted through the cardboard bookshelf
Smelling now forever like sweaty turmeric.

DUTCH TILT:

Shallow euphonies
Aphoristic and impossible to metabolize,
Pacing the buckled cherrywood floor,
Hovering over the relentlessness
Of flood damage,
Clenched scenes of brothers and basements
Whisper junkie,
Sloppy fists,
Subtle incest.

Teeth of puncture wound enlightenment.
The moment of slice-through-layer.
Dampened snap of pulled tape.
Real: slicksmack of tongue.
Dull thud of details.
Lids click on plastic tracks:
Cheap communion wine and Sprite.

Hush the actual.
Iodine tastes like iodine,
Tastes like the memory of iodine.

Metonymic openings
At an oblique angle,
Waterlogged film,
Bathtub projector.
The types of horizon lines
Explained by Film Student Boyfriend
Sleeping sexless on every couch.

*Dysphoria
BOXCAR:

Let it be
Slick-shine,
Fist-full of licorice.

Train tracks of abstinence threaded
Through the ribcage
Of a woman
And covered over
With nonsense graffiti.

The fast words click
Behind her teeth
And blur by,
High-voltage signs
Passed on the way.

Eyes glazed over,
The windowlessness
Of a freight train,
Humming along
Somewhere in the left
Half of her torso.

Some small desire
"To be a woman"
Lays itself down
On the tracks,
Waiting to be
Blinded by the dust-caked
Headlight.

REVISITING: A POEM FROM THE CLOSET:

The ambulance lights
Stain red brick
Red
Through the window,
Crying like a pack of dogs -
Too pathetic to be
A howl -
I am going broke
In this coffee shop,
Afraid of the slam poets,
Begging a God
I don't believe in
For enough ribcage
To build an angry incest poem
And a mic stand,
To pull the brave
Out of battered body,
And "break like Texas,"
To stop scribbling manically
In the backs of borrowed
Levertov books,
To build a church
Out of spines and sound,
To loot its stained glass
Windows like a storefront,
With nervous vibration,
To have a cavalcade
Of teeth,
Enough to spare
In this fistfight
With defiance and dignity.

The rattle in my throat
Shakes off permission
Passed down from a glitter-blooded
Lineage of poets and prophets.
Am I ungrateful,
Snubbing cowboy killers
On their cornerstone,
Sped on sacrament,
Chipping my teeth
On unbreakable bread,
Crushing my bones
Into mortar,

20

Making bricks of the impossible
Muscles in my shoulders
For a staircase
To be climbed
By brash boys
Outside of dive bars,

Praying the gay away
In public restrooms
Where faceless women
In skirts promise privacy
And ignore four
Gospels' worth of blood
From my mother's womb.

MY NOTEBOOK IN YOUR KITCHEN:

Looking, too curious,
Out of windows,
Scanning your mouth
For the taste of lead paint,
I am counting their dreadlocks,
Regrettable stick and poke tattoos,
Sapphic fits on the kitchen floor.

Not a gallery, yet,
Still, the nostalgia arrived early,
Bubble-wrapped carefully
By myself at thirty-five,
With short, bleach-damaged
Brown hair, like dry grass
And premature wrinkles
From reading in the dark
And smoking on the balcony.

This was, I think,
Meant to be a love poem.

SERENITY PRAYER:

The room smells
Like stale coffee
And cigarette breath.
I stand in a circle of strangers' hands
And ask a God
I do not believe in
For "serenity."

I am seven years old
Again and my father
Is on the pulpit.
Breath catches
In my throat
As I am dunked
Into the baptismal pool
And come up,

Gasping, before an audience
Of old women
In their Sunday best:
Embroidered sweaters
With endless pockets
Full of hard candy.

God,
Grant me the serenity
To love a version of you
That is more than anger
In the ether.

God,
Grant me the courage
To bare my soul
When I want
To bare my teeth.

God,
Grant me the wisdom
To stop using
Atheism
As an excuse
To assume
The role of Universal
Choreographer.

Little plastic cups
Passed on a golden tiered tray
Filled with sweet savior blood
Taught me the holiness
Of fermented grapes
That grew their vines
Around my throat,
After I had chosen
Not eat this bread
I could not break
And left the cup of the covenant
In the cabinet
When I lifted bottles
Of Jack from the convenience store
On the corner.

I dragged my body
Like a cross,
All angles
Trying to point
To the place
Where blood freezes
In veins
And becomes brittle.

I try to remind myself
That no one here knows
My father, awake long nights
In his study,
Knows that I have had
The Lord's Prayer memorized
Since I could spell my name,
Notices that I do not
Say the "God" that comes before "grant."

Close your eyes
And feel the salt and sweat
Of their sober palms.

God,
Grant me the serenity
To forget every verse
Of toxic testament,

The courage to build
A lexicon wider
Than the firmament
For "grace",

The wisdom
To find a forgiveness
That subsumes everything
I cannot set free
From useless signifiers
And threatening designations.

DIGNITY IN THE BODY OF REVOLT:

Eat your perfume
through rough days,
when you ask
what was really between the forceps;
mind running over notions
of cold and silver
until you implant a false,
arial-view memory
of your own birth.

"She wasn't shaped,"
commentary says,
"to take that name."
Or else,
"She was and you are not."

Really, it depends on the day,
on what you had for breakfast,
on what you read in the paper,
if you read the paper at all.

This time of year,
we allow for great things

(let the bodies fall where they will)

when Tuesday won't align,
or may not,
wounds become more objective
and I cannot wonder
about purification or symmetry,
but who will be strewn across the sidewalk,
torn at the lip-seam.

And for your gaslight,
here is footage of proximity.
We ask that you ignore the announcers.
(not a sport,
not at play,
not consenting to a subsidized narrative.)

They say silence
is in the very concept of authority,
decibels bolstered up
on the bruised backs of quiet,
Yertle style.

It ends, of course,
with sound.
Autonomy is not a power vacuum
left when coercion and tyranny
crawl away.
It is filled with skin,
fumes sinking into place,
a critique of the duality between dissension and reconciliation.
(not opposites: causes and effects.)

Madness need not be less.
Our doubts are concrete.
Gratitude will take a break
and let them hold our backs.
Stronger than the line.

Henry is painting with stitches,
Becca all drugged up,
while our hours pass
through strangers' eyes.
The bombs, they will say,
were meant to keep us warm.

The morning will be about life:
a hope to metabolize.
This process, we wish,
would follow more closely
on the heels of the tasting.

Time, again,
to think of the forceps
in new light, new weather,
no breakfast,
not knowing much of hope
but vague prayers:

May we approach
the hours of wandering museums,
of a self-forgetting clarity
that doesn't glare so harshly
in the eyes,
of dusty holidays,
questions of sublimity
as a constellation of books and letters
and possibilities of restoration,
possibilities of reinventing the wheel,
digging for the original
and arguing gently and for fun
what came first,
if anything at all,
rather than this pushing
of rocks, all corners
down blocked off streets

ASPIRATION:

We practice walking on our hands,
So that our palms can callous
And we can touch hot stoves
Like children who don't know better,
Only we do
And the innocence,
(Sweet, sloppy, dangerous thing)
Blew out with the candles on your eighth
Birthday cake,
The last time you consumed without
Thinking.

See, gentleness isn't
That way, anymore,
Not the natural, open,
Shag-carpet softness
That ruined us when we were small.
It's labor,
It builds the muscles in your shoulders
Tight.
This tear and shatter thing
Makes you give birth and break rocks,
Makes you work for it.

To wake up every day
And put your back into gentleness
Is to let the lock on your chest
Be picked by strangers
With bobby pins,
Lovers with cold stethoscopes
Listening for the
Click,
Click,
Click.
To wash the streets, smog, sweat
Off of your body,
Slowly,
Like worship,
Like learning braille,
Like learning that it's okay

To give yourself to time
Time to pour honey in your tea,

Time to notice
That your breathing
Still sounds like a chorus of sleeping children,
Time to dig the combination
Out of the drawer of that old desk
In your parents' attic.

The names,
Places,
Shades of sky
That open you up
Still sitting there,
Scrawled in lopsided,
Cautious green crayon
And a sticky note
That says:
Someday, I'll learn to walk on my hands.

ENOUGH:

Not enough care
For the traffic,
She warned me about this:
About busying myself
With words and pictures.

How many times
Am I doomed to return to them?
The one of my father,
Awake in his cluttered study,
Wondering when I learned
To appreciate softness
In between the debris
Of abandoned trajectories:
The life I would've spent
In metropolitan symphonies,
Building churches in the jungle
Of Guatemala,
Wasting away in the brazen embrace
Of inverted narcissism.

My mother:
Sound asleep in the airport lobby,
Lulled by frantic phone calls
To every hotel in San Francisco
With no room for Madonna
And gestating Jesus Christ.

And you:
Improvising softcore porn
For cigarettes
On a crowded frathouse balcony,
Pressing into me impatiently
Until we slide, lifeless,
Onto the air mattress in your living room,
Where you tacitly consent
To falling asleep
In that dress
And brewing coffee
In the slow boredom
Of the morning.

And, still,
I ignore
The traffic.

*Transphobia, Sexual Assault
THAT SIMPLE:

No tectonic shifts.

Half an avocado,

A glass of water,

A nap in an unmade bed,

A dream of my brothers,

Crimes reversed,

Incest becoming a fist,

A fist becoming a hand.

There were open palms

On every street corner

Of my mind,

But none of them seemed

To claim the spill.

Every harbinger

Of emergency

Behind shatter proof glass,

Nothing could rouse them,

Make them bodyguards.

Nothing but this:

A piece of floss stuck in the tired

Beige grout of the tile,

A ring of soap residue lining

The cracked porcelain sink,

A strand of pubic hair

Clinging to the shower curtain.

The thousand boring indignities

Of human beings,

Their careless functioning,

At once universal and secret

In spaces

At once public and private.

Strangers

Rinsing

The froth of their toothpaste,

Their piss,

Their sweat

Down drains.

IN YOUR SLEEP:

Water boils,
Waiting to receive the rose hips.
Why are we sitting in these cramped apartments?
(Is there anything we can't romanticize?)

The dogs woke us up
Three months ago,
Wrestling in the narrow stucco hallway.
(Had I chosen to stay awake because you were so warm?)

Something percolated in us,
Quite possibly the faux stone tiles
Reacting to the scant overhead lighting.
This is what happens when permeability is encouraged.

Three nights of deep sleep
And long-distance phone calls
Brought my brother into the August bedroom
With a thick, sharp mouth full of powder.

The mint garden's low stone wall,
Red plum,
Maps,
Signatures.

If anything crossed over,
Perhaps the fact of two wooden boxes
Holding identical tokens
Stolen from a dry fountain,
Will we continue to forgive each other
For the slow, solidifying details?

COAST GUARD:

I heard they fell somewhere by the cliffs,
Just north of Natural Bridges.
We are all in the business of tragedy.

Seeing the sky
As a cavalcade of bruises,
Marked with trinkets
And trophies from a bar fight,
And tucking it into bed

"I was happy in the haze of a drunken hour,"
My roommate sings to her mother on the phone.

Suppose we practice maternal nurturance
On the inanimate
And the vast,
On all that might do
Just as well
Without our concern

The greyhound bus crashed,
My father, though he wouldn't admit it,
Makes a living saving souls
In a mood-lit nightclub
On River Street,
Where the statue of Uncle Sam
Greets drunken hipsters
Stumbling out of wine bars,
Slurring about feminism.

EDUCATIONAL VARIETY:

"Most of our experiences are what the psychologist William James calls the
"educational variety" because they develop slowly over a period of time."
-Big Book of Alcoholics Anonymous (Appendix II, Spiritual Experience)

Learning: A slow crawl over a dirty rug,
A horizontal shit-show-shimmy
Over layers of dust, skin flakes, and dog hair.
No pride to be taken in the idiot army crawl efforts,
Since the shades are not drawn
And the neighbors may look in,
As you catch the first hints of tight-buttoned shame
And half naked narcissism.

A sweaty heap of half-formed muscle and contradiction,
Several hours of this awkward exertion has brought you
To a coffee stain, a discarded dryer sheet, a reminder of your shot lung
capacity,
Envy for the kensho children on their cushions
Who can inhale the sacred in air-conditioned studios and halls
Where "like pulling teeth" doesn't mean "like pulling your own teeth
With the thread that came off your dirty t-shirt,
Crushing the enamel and snorting that shit
In a stupid attempt to feel like the 'divine in you'
Took a bite out of your frontal lobe."

Nostalgic for the communion of Jack,
The ash tray shrine they call a parking lot,
Vertical existence as a suitable form of worship,
Small, boring, hedonisms as substitutes for surrender
Making a covenant with things as they are,
Here, below the body.

*Eating Disorder
JULIE:

Colorado winters were yours first,
And here I am,
Kamel Reds,
New tattoo,
Nostalgia in the graffiti.

And, as for the truth,
I have not been using
The can opener,
The shower curtains,
And stubborn faucets,
The old soundtrack
To my struggle with gravity.

You are just the same:
On the swing set,
"A fixture,"
As you would say.
And "whatever trips your trigger,"

However many spoonfuls
Of almond butter,
However we measure
The heaviness of plates,
I am sorry
For my dry skin,
For the rust in the locks,
For losing your letter.

My thumb wants
Your hammered silver ring,
All the arthritis in the world,
The pulse point
Of a body that is trying,
Your parking lot ice cream cone.

Golden Colorado
Is a bronzed baby shoe.
No garage sales,
And I am dropping
State quarters into the cold
Hands of street corner caricatures,
Wishing I could teach your daughter
How to play the guitar.

AFTER ALL / FOR LIJE:

I'm building a makeshift home
Out of abandoned cement mixer residue
And scrap metal,
The only way I know how
To ask you to take up cartography
And find some place for yourself
With me
Beyond the penitent kiss
Of these stupid city limits.

I am learning,
Again and slowly,
With my hands,
How to allow for the weather
Without clean socks
And half the dirty tea cups,

Taking every perfect thing
And nurturing it
With pity,
Tucking it into bed
With stories of the French Revolution
Or excerpts from my book
Of ransom notes,
Loveletters,
And unfinished eulogies.

I will keep myself busy
With sparse architecture,
While you begin your clumsy map
With a dry brush.

* Alcoholism, sexual assault
# ANACHRONISMS PT 2:

The world doubled over,
Mint and drenched,
A deluge of telephone wire tennis shoes,
Cigarette butt shrines
On the corner of 31st and Folsom,
Reconstructed details,
Scraps of episodic fallacy
And composite memory
Littering the sidewalks
In front of boarded up coffee shop windows,
Mimicking the way of skin,
Becoming molten in soft lighting,
In the final remnants of urban lack.
Street lights showed them up
Until they reflected potential forest fire.

"The light takes the tree,"
But here it is a rape,
Rather than an instance
Of sublimity,
Fuck off Yeats,
We already killed God,
Nice and slow,
No bullet holes of light,
With the regrettable
Smallness of each abrasion
That comes from an anger
Meant to be reckless and consuming,
In the ten minutes passed
In the first-hit sway and hum
Of cheap whiskey,
No sweeter for the theft.

Before nausea sets in,
The world is with us and plenty,
As what was not enough
Becomes too much,
As each dull shade of drywall
Awakens sleeper agents
In the cornea,
Eats shit climbing the grey scale,
Searing and biting, in turn.

Morning After:
All the things that buckle
(Sensibilities,
insulation,
tooth enamel)
Under stress,
With changes in temperature,
Anything abrupt, really,
The oracles and debutantes
Sat down in the back lot
Of the millionth bed and breakfast
In town and tried in vain
To compile a list,
Alphabetically,
Getting stuck somewhere around
"Composure,"
All agreeing that was the sum
But not sure how to break it
Down into parts.

The steeple cast sundial shadows,
Assuring them that God was late,
Or, really,
They were early.

Leibniz called to tell me
That it was all for the best.
Too bad my phone was dead
In someone else's apartment
In Denver.

* Alcoholism
# HOW YOU WAKE TUESDAY MORNING:

Your shadow is towering
In the parking lot,
Hovering over your shoulders,
Begging you to look back
On the shattered bottles
Littering the curb,
To kneel and lick
The last sharp fragments
Of whiskey off the concrete,
To ignore the tricks
Of street lamps -
How they glitter-fuck
Every chromatic outline
Of who you've been.

You are praying to the ghosts of the living,
The way children do:
Supplications to Kathleen Hanna,
To the last dealer
You went blow for blow with,
To the first woman
Who made a man out of you.

You are calling down specters again:
Begging their shapes
To emerge
From the light cast
Through the fire escape.
You are praying to the dead
For once:
Pleading them out
Of coffins and ceramics,
Up from the ground,
Off of the mantlepiece,
Convincing yourself
Of the phantom limbs
Around the vacant space

Of your torso;

Brooke with those eyes

Like agates
Hums Suzanne Vega
In your ear.
The smallest blue things lock
Into your shadow cochlea,
Somehow unchanged
By the shifting skylight.

You stay
Until the whiskey dries up,
The night evaporates,
The sun swallows
Your shadow whole
In its hot mouth.

You stay
Until logic takes back your skin,
Until you feel the hollow exit wound
Of prayer in your cheek,
Until you are so self-referential
You could swear
You see the ghost of T.S. Eliot
Wink at you in the window glare
Of the coffee shop
Opening across the street.

*Psychiatric abuse/general trauma
HOW YOU SLEEP WEDNESDAY NIGHT

PART ONE or REMEMBER WHEN YOU FOUND THAT BIRD ON
THE SIDEWALK WHEN YOU WERE LIKE ELEVEN AND YOU
TRIED TO SAVE IT AND YOU COULDN'T AND EVERYONE
THOUGHT YOU'D START CRYING BUT YOU JUST SAID SOME
WEIRD SHIT ABOUT THE LAW OF CONSERVATION OF
MATTER AND STARTED GRINDING YOUR JAW AGAIN UNTIL
YOUR MOM TOOK YOU TO THE DENTIST AND GOT YOU
FITTED FOR A MOUTH GUARD?:

The way you carry yourself
Has convinced them
You are tall.
Five feet of frame and your sister
Describes you as
"Towering,"

Has come to consider
The fourteen inches she imagined
Above your head
To be the phantom height
Of having grown the size of your grief.

Your ninth therapist said
You would need to eat
Before you could lift your fear
From that sunken chest
For her dissection,
"Trauma is so heavy.
It's okay that you can't carry it yet."

Countless corpse brides
Looked out at you from their deadened,
Dripping drugged eyes
In their folding plastic group chairs
And said things like,
"Worried they would be crushed
if I told them,"
And,"It's so much, I just drown in it."

Maybe that is true.
Maybe the story that Emily's mind

43

Told her every night while she slept
Thrashing in the cot next to yours
On the adolescent unit
Crushed her parents
Like a player piano
Out a sixteen-story window.

Maybe Charlotte's lungs
Filled with fists
When she dove into the one-way
Bar brawl of her drunken stepbrother.

Maybe that ninth therapist
Toned and built muscles
Out of corn-husk dolls
Slumped into her couch cushions
Until they could lift
The monster trucks of their trauma
From the ditches of their denial.

But you remember the first time,
The only time you ever held something
As small and warm and soft
As your grief,
As the fear that makes nests
In the branches of your ribcage:
Seven hours old,
Fallen from a tree
In that storm that took out your power
For two weeks;
How you wrapped it in your jacket
And carried it home.
Afraid to drop something
Not even solid enough to shatter.

PART TWO or GET IT TOGETHER AND START LOSING YOUR SHIT
ALREADY:

When you are told
You have grown the size of your grief,
You want to say that you've grown
The size of your silence,
The size of the cogs
That grind your denial
Into the lies you tell yourself
To fall asleep at night,
Or the truths you pretend to understand.

44

It is easy to grow.
You've built twenty-two years
Worth of a boi's body
From the quiet, slow whispers
Of a girl's hunger.
You've built bloated bookshelves
From the four-letter words
You still can't say out loud.
You've built totalitarian gods
From pocket bibles.

Darling,
If trauma were stick-shift,
Long highway,
Ocean,
Solid wood, and
Ivory,
Tower:
Mechanic-grease and erase
The town you broke down in from every map,
Plumb its depths with an oxygen tank
Strapped obligation-heavy to your back,
Cut it down,
Become the smoothest
Swing of an axe.

But Darling,
It is so small
That if you ever grew
The size of your grief,
You wouldn't even be big enough
To snap between fingers,
You might just disappear.

So you do not come
To your grief
With elbow grease and wrench
And tear it wheel from axel,
To your fear with a wetsuit and a mask,
To your shame with moving vans and piano tuners,
To your memories with strong jaws and phantom stature.

You come with a blanket,
Shaking palms,
Strip down,
Kneel,
Believe that someday you will grow
The size of your patience,

The size of your humility,
The size of yourself.

Despite what they've told you,
You will not be
"Brave,"
Brandished bare knuckles
Colliding with the jaws of your ghosts.

You will be gentle:
Open hand over your chest,
Waiting for the subtle ache,
Breathing so quietly
You could hear a pin drop in a hurricane,
Inventing antonyms for "brace yourself,"
Living every memoir of "good survivor"
Cover-to-cover in reverse:

The "moved on and life is beautiful!" stage,
The "atrocities are mud for the lotus!" stage,
The drunken-rages-stage,
The coy-stoicism-stage,
The lanugoed-neophyte stage,
The jagged-confusion stage,
The repressed-numbness-of-pretending-normalcy stage,
And finally,
The tiny limbs of trust and betrayal
Tangled on the floor of your mother's house,
The fresh shame scratching at your corneas,
The first broken moment of helplessness,
So soft you couldn't even break with the bough,

And a revision:
You stop trying to.
You bruise like flesh,
Skin a storm warning.
You cry like your life depends on it.
Because it does.

ABOUT THE AUTHOR'S DOG:

Huxley Punko Radish is a two-year-old mastiff pit bull rescue puppy who lives at the raddest co-op in Colorado. He enjoys peanut butter, tree branches, and headbutting his human, Blake. Huxley is an avid collector of dirt and debris. His current titles include Prince of Darkness, Constable Mayor, Hunksley, Small Punk, Baby Pig, Borkador, Boopus, Man Candy, Beefcake, and Little Bunny. In his spare time, he barks at strangers, friends, family members, and the things that only he can see. Huxley was a key factor in the composition of As for the Body, spending countless nights eating Cheetos in bed with Blake.

ALSO FROM PUNCH DRUNK PRESS

```
UPID_FLOWERS_STUPI
D_FLOWERS_STUPID_
FLOWERS_STUPID_FL
OWERS_STUPID_FLO
WERS_STUPID_FLOWE
RS_STUPID_FLOWERS
_STUPID_FLOWERS_S
TUPID_FLOWERS_STU
PID_FLOWERS_STUPID
_FLOWERS_POEMS_F
LOWERS_STUPID_FLO
WERS_STUPID_FLOWE
RS_BRICE_MAIURRO_
STUPID_FLOWERS_ST
UPID_FLOWERS_STUPI
D_FLOWERS_STUPID
```

Stupid Flowers
Poems by Brice Maiurro
Released June 2017

"In a playful, often humorous way, Maiurro effortlessly draws on the strange, the surreal, and sometimes the intangible to create the most beautiful and magical imagery." -Ann Reads Them

WWW.PUNCHDRUNKPRESS.COM

www.ingramcontent.com/pod-product-compliance
Lightning Source LLC
Chambersburg PA
CBHW031215090426

42736CB00009B/933